Ivan Sergeevich Turgenev

**Poems in Prose**

Ivan Sergeevich Turgenev

**Poems in Prose**

ISBN/EAN: 9783744689014

Printed in Europe, USA, Canada, Australia, Japan

Cover: Foto ©Thomas Meinert / pixelio.de

More available books at **www.hansebooks.com**

Yours very truly,
Ivan Tourguéneff.

# POEMS IN PROSE

BY

IVAN TOURGUÉNEFF

BOSTON
CUPPLES, UPHAM AND COMPANY
1883

ELECTROTYPED.

BOSTON STEREOTYPE FOUNDRY,
4 PEARL STREET.

# TOURGUÉNEFF.

To his keen, melancholy glance lay bare
   The throbbing heart of Russia, — fierce, intense,
   Primeval passion, firing soul and sense
Of serf and noble, — Mumu's sad, dumb care, —
The eager young men's thoughts, who madly dare
   To think and die for thought's sake, — the immense
   Oppression of the empire, and the dense
Child-minded millions whom no emperors spare.

This has he seen and written as he saw,
   And in that barbarous, ice-bound land revealed,
     A century in twenty years unrolled,
And writ in words of fire life's changeless law
   Of human rights, eternal, unrepealed,
     That nations on their knees have learned of old.

# PREFACE.

This little volume contains a translation of what are among the last things written by Tourguéneff. They are best defined by the title that he half suggested for them, — Poems in Prose; for, while their form is that of prose, the subjects, the treatment, the imaginative setting, have all the charm and quality of poetry. It is believed that the reader will find enough beauty, pathos, and vividness in these pieces to pardon the inevitable pallor of a translation. This has at least been made with the utmost respect for the work of one of the greatest of our contemporaries.

As to the poems themselves, they are of very different kinds. Some are like studies for the scenes of a novel; others, again, like a conversation, are purely imaginative sketches, while yet others, it is safe to conjecture, have an autobiographic interest. All bear the deep impressions of his wonderful genius. Even the slightest of them will repay study; for, just as the writer in natural history can only acquire a full comprehension of the majesty of nature by the careful investigation of what to the careless seem trifles, so human nature is only to be known by the careful and sympathetic observance of the slightest acts and feelings. The reader will be led to doubt some of the current statements about Tourguéneff; one, which he himself is said have expressed, is, that he lacked imagination. If by this it is meant that he could never satisfy himself with drawing vague types, but was always compelled to keep touch with truth that might be verified by observation, the statement is true. But this is very far from affirming that because he was exact, he was not imaginative. One might as well say that Darwin was not a great philosopher, and assign as a reason that he studied earthworms.

Another unwarrantable statement is, that Tourguéneff lacked sympathy. Are we, then, to suppose that his exposition of the dangers of serfdom was a commercial speculation, — that the comprehension of the weaknesses of his countrymen was cynicism? Fortunately Tourguéneff's readers do not need to have the assertion combated.

As to this little book, Tourguéneff said: "The reader must not skim over these poems in prose one after the other; that would probably tire him, and he would soon cast the book aside. But let him read each one separately, — one to-day, another to-morrow, and then perhaps one or more of them may sink into his soul and bear fruit."

# CONTENTS.

|  | PAGE |
|---|---|
| THE VILLAGE | 11 |
| THE OLD WOMAN | 15 |
| A DIALOGUE | 19 |
| THE DOG | 22 |
| MY OPPONENT | 23 |
| AN AXIOM | 25 |
| DOST THOU HEARKEN TO THE WORDS OF THE FOOL | 26 |
| THE BEGGAR | 28 |
| A CONTENTED MAN | 30 |
| THE DESTRUCTION OF THE WORLD | 31 |
| MASCHA | 35 |
| THE BLOCKHEAD | 38 |
| AN ORIENTAL LEGEND | 41 |
| TWO QUATRAINS | 45 |
| THE SPARROW | 50 |
| THE LABORER AND THE MAN WITH THE WHITE HAND | 52 |
| THE SKULL | 54 |
| THE LAST MEETING | 56 |
| THE ROSE | 58 |
| THE VISIT | 61 |
| NECESSITAS · VIS · LIBERTAS | 63 |
| THE ALMS | 64 |
| THE INSECT | 67 |
| THE CABBAGE-SOUP | 69 |

## CONTENTS.

| | |
|---|---|
| THE HAPPY LAND | 71 |
| WHO IS THE RICHER | 74 |
| THE OLD MAN | 75 |
| THE NEWSPAPER CORRESPONDENT | 76 |
| TWO BROTHERS | 77 |
| IN MEMORY OF L. P. W. | 80 |
| THE EGOTIST | 82 |
| THE SUPREME BEING'S BANQUET | 85 |
| THE NYMPHS | 86 |
| THE SPHINX | 90 |
| THE FRIEND AND THE ENEMY | 92 |
| CHRIST | 94 |
| THE STONE | 96 |
| THE DOVES | 97 |
| TO-MORROW, TO-MORROW! | 100 |
| NATURE | 101 |
| "HANG HIM!" | 103 |
| WHAT SHALL I THINK ABOUT? | 107 |
| "HOW LOVELY AND FRESH THOSE ROSES WERE!" | 108 |
| A TRIP BY SEA | 111 |
| N. N. | 114 |
| STOP! | 115 |
| THE MONK | 116 |
| LET'S KEEP A GOOD HEART | 117 |
| PRAYER | 119 |
| THE RUSSIAN LANGUAGE | 120 |

# POEMS IN PROSE.

## THE VILLAGE.

It is the last day of July: for a thousand versts on every side lies Russia, — home.

The whole sky is a shadowless blue; one little cloud only floats upon it and melts away. A windless, sultry calm; the air like warm milk.

The larks trill, the doves coo, the swallows sweep by with their swift and noiseless flight; the horses neigh and crop the grass; the dogs stand about, gently wagging their tails, but not barking.

There is a mingled smell of smoke, hay, tar, and leather.

The hemp is ripe, and gives forth its penetrating but pleasant odor.

In a deep, gently-sloping ravine grow rows of thick-topped, weather-beaten willows. Below them flows a brook; in its bed the stones quiver beneath the rippling surface of the water. In the distance, where earth and sky join, is to be seen the blue line of a broad river.

On one side of the ravine are a number of neat little barns and storehouses, their doors all carefully closed; on the other side, half a dozen peasants' huts built of fir logs and boards. Every roof is surmounted by a bird-house on the top of a tall pole; on the gables are tin horses' heads with stiff manes. The rough panes of glass shimmer with all the colors of the rainbow. On the window-shutters are vases of flowers painted in a very primitive fashion. Before the houses stand heavy benches, with here and there a cat curled up in a ball, with pointed, transparent ears; behind the high threshold is the cool, dark interior.

I am lying on a horse-blanket close to the

edge of the ravine, amid scattered heaps of the fragrant new-mown hay. The busy peasants have spread the hay out before the houses, that it may dry in the summer sun; then it goes into the barn; — it is delightful to sleep upon.

Curly-headed children peep out from under heaps of hay; busy hens pick about after beetles and flies; a young dog is rolling on the grass.

Brown-haired lads in long, white blouses, belted at the waist, and with heavy boots on, are leaning against a cart and laughing together, and chaffing one another.

A young, round-faced woman looks out of the window, and laughs half at the boys and half at the children frolicking in the hay.

Another young woman is drawing with her stout arms a great dripping bucket out of the well. The bucket sways and trembles on the rope and lets fall long, sparkling drops.

An old woman is standing before me;

she has on a new checked dress and new leather shoes.

Three rows of large glass beads encircle her withered, sunburnt throat; her gray hair is covered with a red and yellow-striped kerchief, which hangs low over her dull eyes.

But the old eyes smile pleasantly, the whole of her wrinkled face smiles, the old creature must be nearly eighty years old. . . . Yet one can still see that she was beautiful as a girl.

The brown claw-like fingers of her right hand hold a cup which is full of cold milk, fresh from the cellar. The outside of the cup is covered with drops of moisture. On the palm of her left hand she reaches out to me a large slice of fresh black bread,— "Eat, and may it do you good!"

Suddenly the cock crows and claps his wings; answered soon by the bleating of a calf from the barn. "I call that cheeky," I hear my coachman say.

This contentment, this rest and plenty in a free Russian village! Oh, this blessed quiet!

And I think to myself: What is the need of a cross on the Church of Santa Sophia of Constantinople, and all that sort of thing, that we city-people think so much of?

FEBRUARY, 1878.

––◆––

## THE OLD WOMAN.

I WAS walking alone through a broad field. Suddenly it seemed to me as if I heard behind me a light, cautious footfall. Some one was following me.

I looked round — I saw a little, bent old woman bundled up in gray rags. Nothing but the face — a yellow, wrinkled, sharp-nosed, toothless face — was to be seen.

I stepped up to her . . . she stood still.

— "Who are you? What do you want? Are you a beggar? Do you want alms?"

The old woman did not answer. I bent down to her, and noticed that both her eyes were covered by a half-transparent, white film, such as some birds have as protection against too bright a light.

But on this old woman's eyes the film was immovable; it never left the pupil . . . whence I concluded that she was blind.

— "Do you want money?" I repeated. "Why do you follow me?" Still the old woman answered not, but stooped a little more.

I turned and went on my way.

And again I heard the same light, even, creeping step behind me.

— "There's that woman again!" thought I;—"what does she want of me?" But it at once occurred to me that probably she had got lost on account of her blindness, and was now guiding herself by her hearing, following my steps that I might lead her to an inhabited neighborhood. . . . Yes, yes, that is it! . . . But a strange unrest took possession of me. . . . It seemed to me as if this old woman was not following me, but was driving me where she wished to go, as if she made me turn now to the right, now to the left, and as if I involuntarily obeyed her.

Nevertheless I go on and on . . . until something black appears in my path, just before me; it grows larger, it is a hole. "A grave!" The thought flashed through my head. Thither was she driving me.

I turn short about. The old woman is again before me, — but no longer blind. She looks at me with large, evil, threatening eyes, — the eyes of a bird of prey. . . . I lean closer to her face, to her eyes, . . . there was again that dingy skin, there was again that dull, blind look.

"Ah!" think I, "this old woman is my fate, — fate, which no man may escape."

"No escape? Not escape? — what madness! One should at least try!" and I start in another direction.

I hasten . . . but the soft tread rustles behind me, near, very near . . . and before me is again the dark grave.

I turn once more, — and again comes the same rustling behind me, the same dark spot appears before me.

As I turn hither and thither like a hunted hare, . . . it is always the same, always the same.

Stop, think I, I will outwit her. I will stay here, — and suddenly I sit down on the ground.

The old woman is standing two steps behind me. I do not hear her, but feel that she is there.

And suddenly I see: that dark spot that was visible in the distance floats, creeps up towards me!

God! . . . I look around. . . . The old woman looks fixedly at me, and her toothless mouth is distorted with a smile. . . .

— "Thou canst not escape me!"

FEBRUARY, 1878.

## A DIALOGUE.

The Alpine summits — a complete chain of steep precipices, right in the heart of the Alps. Over the mountains is a pale-green, clear, silent sky. Hard, biting frost; firm, sparkling snow; dark, weather-beaten, ice-bound crags rise from beneath the snow.

Two colossi, two giants, rise from the horizon on either side, — the Jungfrau and the Finsteraarhorn.

And the Jungfrau asks her neighbor: "What is the news? You can see better; what is going on down there?"

Thousands of years pass by — as one moment. And Finsteraarhorn thunders back the answer: "Impenetrable clouds veil the earth . . . wait!"

Again, thousands of years pass — as one moment.

— "Well, what now?" asks the Jungfrau.

— "Now! see: everything there is unchanged, confused, and petty. Blue water, dark woods, heaped up masses of gray stone, with those little insects running all about, you know, — the two-legged ones which have never yet ventured to intrude upon your summit or mine."

— "Men?" — "Yes, men."

Again, thousands of years pass by — as a moment.

— "Well, what now?" asks the Jungfrau.

— "It seems to me as if fewer of those insects are to be seen," thunders Finsteraarhorn; — "it's getting clearer down there, — the waters narrower, the woods thinner!"

Again, thousands of years pass by — like one moment.

— "What do you see now?" asks the Jungfrau.

— "Round about us, near by, it seems to have got clearer," answered Finsteraarhorn; "but down there, in the distance, in the valleys there are still some spots, and something moving."

— "And now?" asks the Jungfrau, after thousands of years more — a mere moment.

— "Now all is well," answered Finsteraarhorn; — "clear and shining everywhere: pure white wherever you look. . . . Our snow everywhere, nothing but snow and ice. All is frozen. All is calm and peaceful."

— "Yes, now it is well!" answers the Jungfrau; "but we have talked enough, old friend. Let us sleep awhile."

— "Yes, it is time we did."

They sleep, the giant mountains. The clear green sky too sleeps above the ever-silent earth.

FEBRUARY, 1878.

## THE DOG.

THERE are two of us in the room, my dog and I. Outside, a fearful storm is raging.

The dog is sitting in front of me and gazing straight into my eyes. I too am looking into his eyes.

It seems to me as if he longed to say something to me. He is mute, dumb, has no understanding of himself, — but I understand him.

I understand that the same feeling lives in him as in myself, that there is no difference between us. We are alike; in each of us glows and burns the same flickering flame.

Death is approaching, — a single blow from his cold, mighty wing . . . and that is the end!

Who can distinguish then the special flame that glows in each of us?

No! it was not man and animal that

were looking at each other. It was two pairs of eyes of the same kind which were fixed on each other; and in each of these pairs of eyes, the beast's as well as the man's, it is the same life appealing to the other.

FEBRUARY, 1878.

---

## MY OPPONENT.

I HAD a comrade who was my opponent, not, to be sure, in our studies, work, or love; — but our ways of looking at things were wholly inharmonious, and every time we met an endless strife was kindled between us.

We disputed about everything, — art, religion, knowledge; about life on this earth and life after death, — especially the latter.

He was an enthusiast and a believer. Once he said to me: "You make fun of everything; but if I die before you do I will come back from the other world and appear to you ... then we shall see whether you will laugh."

And sure enough he did die before me while he was yet young; a long time went by,—and I forgot his promise, his threat.

One night I was lying in bed, and could not sleep.

The chamber was neither light nor quite dark; I was gazing into the gray half-light.

Suddenly it seemed to me as if my opponent stood between the two windows, and gently, sadly, nodded his head.

I was not frightened, nor even surprised ... but raised myself slightly on my arm, and looked at the strange apparition.

It continued nodding.

—"Well," I said at last, "do you come in triumph or in pity? What does this mean? A warning or a reproach? Or do you tell me that you were wrong, or that we both were wrong? What do you feel?—the pangs of Hell?—the joys of Paradise? Tell me ... just one word!"

But my opponent uttered no sound; he only nodded sadly and submissively.

I laughed aloud,— and he vanished.

FEBRUARY, 1878.

## AN AXIOM.

"IF you wish really to vex and injure your opponent," said an old diplomatist to me once, "just accuse him of the fault, the vice of which you yourself are guilty; — pretend to be angry, and reproach him with it sharply.

"In the first place, you thereby convince others that you are innocent of this fault.

"In the second place, your indignation may even be genuine. You profit through the reproaches of your own conscience."

"If you are a renegade, for instance, accuse your opponent of want of sound faith!

"If you are a snob, find fault with him for snobbishness; accuse him of being a cultured, socialist snob.

"One might even say he was an anti-snob-snob!" I remarked.

"Yes, you might indeed!" acquiesced the diplomatist.

FEBRUARY, 1878.

―――♦―――

## "DOST THOU HEARKEN TO THE WORDS OF THE FOOL?"— PUSHKIN.

"Dost thou hearken to the words of the fool?" You have ever spoken truly, you, our sublimest singer; and this time also.

"The words of the fool and the laughter of the many!" . . . Who does not know them by experience?

All this one can and should bear; and, if he be strong enough, even despise it.

There are blows which are far more painful . . . One man did all that he could; he worked with all his strength, zealously and honestly . . . And yet "honorable souls" turn from him with horror; "honorable people" blush at the mere mention of his name. "Get out of the way! Be off!" "honorable" young voices call to him. "We want neither you nor your works; you defile our dwelling—you neither know nor understand us . . . You are our enemy!"

What should this man do? . . . He should continue to work, he should make no attempt to justify himself. He should never expect to be judged justly.

The peasants at first cursed the foreigner who brought them the potato,—that daily food of the poor, a substitute for bread . . . They tore the precious gifts from his outstretched hands, threw them in the mud, and stamped on them.

Now they live on them, and do not know even the name of their benefactor.

No matter! What's in a name? Although unknown, he has saved them from starvation.

Let us only make sure that what we bring them is really nutritious food.

Bitter is unjust reproof from the mouths of those whom we love . . . Yet even this may be borne.

"Strike — but hear me!" said the Athenian to the Spartan.

"Strike, but grow healthy and strong!" we must say.

FEBRUARY, 1878.

---

## THE BEGGAR.

I WAS walking in the street . . . a beggar stopped me, — a frail old man.

His inflamed, tearful eyes, blue lips, rough rags, disgusting sores . . . oh, how horribly poverty had disfigured the unhappy creature!

He stretched out to me his red, swollen, filthy hand . . . he groaned and whimpered for alms.

I felt in all my pockets . . . no purse,

watch, or handkerchief did I find. I had left them all at home.

The beggar waited... and his outstretched hand twitched and trembled slightly.

Embarrassed and confused, I seized his dirty hand and pressed it... "Don't be vexed with me, brother; I have nothing with me, brother."

The beggar raised his bloodshot eyes to mine; his blue lips smiled, and he returned the pressure of my chilled fingers.

— "Never mind, brother," stammered he; "thank you for this — this, too, was a gift, brother."

I felt that I, too, had received a gift from my brother.

FEBRUARY, 1878.

## A CONTENTED MAN.

A YOUNG man is mincing along the streets of the capital. His manner is contented, cheerful, and self-conscious; his eyes are sparkling, his lips smiling, and his pretty little face is slightly flushed. He looks the picture of contented self-satisfaction.

What has happened to him? Has he received a legacy? Has he come into a title? Is his lady-love waiting for him? or is it merely a feeling of physical comfort and satisfaction, the result of a good breakfast, that pervades his whole body? or has he, perhaps, had hung about his neck the beautiful eight-cornered cross of the Order of the Polish King, Stanislaus.\*

No, he has only invented and carefully circulated a nice bit of scandal about one of

---

\* A Russian order of moderate importance.

his acquaintances. This scandal then came back to him through some one else, and he has believed it himself.

Oh, how pleased and satisfied is this amiable, promising young man now!

FEBRUARY, 1878.

## THE DESTRUCTION OF THE WORLD.

### A DREAM.

I DREAM that I am in a peasant's hut in some obscure corner of Russia.

The room is large and low, with three windows, whitewashed walls, and very little furniture. In front of the house stretches a broad plain which loses itself in the far distance, over which hangs like a roof a monotonous gray sky.

I am not alone; there are about ten men in the room, very simple, plainly-dressed people; they move silently, as it were gliding to and fro, avoiding each other, but continually casting anxious glances at one another.

None of them know how they came there or what sort of people the others are. Anxiety and depression are to be read on every face; they all step in turn to the windows, and look as if expecting something.

Then they turn again and wander restlessly up and down. A little boy who is among them moans from time to time in a thin, monotonous voice: "Papa, I'm afraid!" This whimpering fairly makes me sick. I too am beginning to be afraid, — but of what? I do not know; I merely feel that some terrible misfortune is approaching.

The little boy goes on whimpering. Oh, if we could only get away from here! How close it is, how sultry, how oppressive . . . but escape is impossible.

The sky is like a pall, there is not the slightest breeze, the air seems dead.

Suddenly the boy calls from the window

with a terrified voice: "Look, look! the earth has fallen away."

What! Fallen away? . . . It is a fact; there had been a plain in front of the house; now it stands on the summit of an enormous mountain! The horizon has fallen down, sunk away; and close to the house yawns a steep, black, gaping abyss!

We all press round the window . . . our hearts stand still with fear. "Look there! — there," whispers my neighbor.

Now over the whole, wide, boundless waste, suddenly something begins to move as if little round hills were rising and falling.

The ocean! — we all thought at once. It will engulf us. But how can that be? How can it rise in its might to the height of this lofty summit?

Meanwhile, it rises ever higher and higher. Now there are not merely little hills visible here and there in the distance . . . A single mighty, monstrous wave sweeps across the whole circle of the horizon.

It is flying towards us! Like an icy whirlwind, it approaches, circling like a dark abyss of Hell. Everything about begins to tremble; and there, in that hurrying chaos, a thousand-voiced, brazen clangor crashes and thunders and roars.

Ah! what howling and groaning! It is the earth, moaning with terror.

Its end has come! Universal destruction!

The little boy goes on whimpering . . . I turn to cling to my companions; but suddenly we are all overwhelmed, buried, drowned, swept away by that pitch-black, icy, monstrous wave.

Darkness — eternal darkness!

Almost breathless, I awake.

MARCH, 1878.

## MASCHA.

MANY years ago, when I was living in St. Petersburg, whenever I hired a droschky, or sleigh, I used to talk with the driver.

I liked especially to chat with the night-drivers, — with those poor peasants from the suburbs, who, with their rackety, yellow painted sleighs and wretched horses, hope to earn enough to support themselves, and pay their *obrok* to their masters.

Once I was riding with such a driver. . . . He was a young man, about twenty years old, tall, well-shaped, a powerfully built fellow with blue eyes and rosy cheeks; brown curls came down over his eyebrows beneath his knit cap. It was a wonder how his ragged coat held together across his broad shoulders.

His smooth, handsome face looked sad and gloomy.

I began to talk to him. Even his voice sounded sad. "Why are you not more cheerful, brother?" I asked him. "Is anything the matter with you?"

He did not answer immediately.

At last, he broke out with: "Yes, sir, I have a sorrow,— such a sorrow as I would not wish to my worst enemy. My wife is dead."

"You loved her, then?"

The fellow did not turn round, but merely nodded his head.

"Yes, sir,— I did love her. . . . It was eight years ago . . . and I cannot get over it. It is gnawing my very heart out . . . all the time. And why should she have died? She was young and strong. But the cholera carried her off in a day."

"She was a good wife to you?"

"Oh, sir,"— the poor fellow sighed deeply, —"we were so fond of each other! She died when I was away. I heard that she was already buried, and I hurried home to the village. When I got there, it was past midnight. I went into my cottage, stood still in the middle of the room, and whispered softly, 'Mascha, oh, Mascha!'... but only the cricket chirped. Then I began to cry, sat down on the ground, and struck the earth with my hands. 'Insatiable maw,' said I, ' you have swallowed her ... swallow me too!'"... "Oh, Mascha!—Mascha!"... added he once more in low tones, and without dropping the reins, wiped a tear from his eyes with his gloved fist, shook it off, shrugged his shoulders, and said not another word.

As I got down, I paid him more than his fare. He pulled off his cap with both hands and made me a low bow, and then drove slowly away over the deserted, snow-covered streets through the gray mists of January.

APRIL, 1878.

## THE BLOCKHEAD.

ONCE upon a time there was a blockhead.

He lived for a long time happy and contented, until at last it came to his ears that he was considered a brainless fool. That stirred him up and worried him. He considered what would be the best way to give the lie to these rumors. Suddenly an idea came into his dull head, and he immediately carried it out.

An acquaintance met him in the street, and praised a famous painter.

"In heaven's name," exclaimed the blockhead, "don't you know that that painter has been thrown into the dust-heap long ago? You must have known that! You are dreadfully behind the times."

His acquaintance was surprised, but at once accepted the blockhead's opinion.

"I have been reading such a delightful book to-day!" said some one else to him.

"Mercy on us!" cried the blockhead, "are you not ashamed of yourself? That is an absolutely worthless book,—there is but one opinion about it. Didn't you know that? What an old fogey you are!"

And this person was overawed too, and agreed with the blockhead.

"Waht a splendid fellow my friend A. is!" said a third acquaintance to the blockhead; "a really fine man!"

"Heavens!" exclaimed the blockhead; "A. is a notorious rascal! He has cheated all his relatives. Is there any one who doesn't know that? How behind the times you are!"

His interlocutor was put down, and at once came over to the blockhead's opinion. Whatever or whoever was praised in his presence, the blockhead had always the same answer ready, and always added reproachfully,— "And do you still go by the authorities?"

"A disagreeable, malicious fellow!" the blockhead was now pronounced by common consent. "But what a head he has!" "And what a tongue!" added others; "oh, he's an able fellow!"

The end of it was that the editor of a paper entrusted the critical part of his paper to the blockhead, who criticised everything and everybody in his favorite fashion, with his well-known remarks. And now he, the former enemy of all authorities, has become an authority himself, and young people respect him greatly and tremble before him.

How can they help it, poor fools?

## AN ORIENTAL LEGEND.

Who in Bagdad does not know great Jaffar, the sun of the universe?

Once, many years ago, when Jaffar was a youth, he was walking in the neighborhood of Bagdad.

Suddenly he heard a hoarse cry, some one calling for help.

Jaffar was distinguished among his companions for wise judgment and lofty understanding, but he had also a sympathetic heart. and could depend upon his strength.

He hastened in the direction of the call, and saw a weak old man crowded against the city wall by two highwaymen, who were about to rob him.

Jaffar drew his sabre and attacked the rascals; one he killed and one he put to flight.

The old man whom he had saved fell at

the feet of his deliverer, kissed the hem of his garment, and exclaimed, "Brave youth! your generosity shall not go unrewarded. I appear to be a miserable beggar; but appearances are deceitful. I am no ordinary man. Come to-morrow at daybreak to the market-place; I will wait for you there at the fountain, and you shall be convinced of the truth of my words."

Jaffar considered: "This man really seems to be only a beggar; — but who knows? Why should I not make the trial?" and he answered and said: "Well, father, I will come!"

The old man looked at him and went away.

The next morning, at daybreak, Jaffar betook him to the market-place. The old man was already waiting for him, leaning against the marble basin of the fountain.

He took Jaffar silently by the hand and led him into a little garden, which was surrounded by a high wall.

In the middle of this garden from the greensward grew a peculiar kind of tree.

It looked like a cypress; but had deep blue leaves. Three apples hung from the stiff, erect boughs, — one, a middling-sized apple, was oval and milk-white; another, large, round, and bright-red; the third, small, wrinkled, and yellow.

The tree rustled softly, although no breeze was blowing. It tinkled gently, as if it were made of glass; and it seemed to be conscious of Jaffar's approach.

"Young man!" said the old man, "pluck one of these apples, and know that if you pluck the white one and eat it, you will become wiser than all other men; if you pluck the red one and eat it, you will become as rich as the Rothschilds; but if you pluck the yellow one and eat it, you will win the favor of all old women. Decide without delay; in one hour, the fruit will wither and the tree sink into the depths of the earth!"

Jaffar bowed his head and considered.

"How shall I decide?" he muttered to himself. "If I am too wise, my life may be miserable. If I become richer than everybody else, that may excite envy, — so I will pluck and eat the third apple!"

He did so, and the old man laughed with his toothless mouth, and said, "Oh, wisest of young men! You have chosen rightly! Why should you want the white apple? You are already wiser than Solomon. The red apple you don't need either; you will become rich without its aid, and yet excite no one's envy."

"Now tell me, venerable old man," said Jaffar, trembling with joy, "where the esteemed mother of our gracious Caliph lives."

The old man bowed low and showed the young man the way there.

Who in Bagdad does not know the sun of the universe, — the great, the celebrated Jaffar?

APRIL, 1878.

## TWO QUATRAINS.

THERE was once a city, the inhabitants of which were such passionate admirers of poetry, that if a few weeks went by without bringing to light new and fine poems, they regarded such poetic unfruitfulness as a public calamity.

Then they would put on their worst clothes, strew their heads with ashes, and assemble in the public squares to lament, shed tears, and bitterly murmur against the Muse for deserting them.

On one such day of mourning there appeared once a youthful poet, Junius, among the sorrowing people in the crowded square.

Quickly he mounted the tribune and signified that he wished to recite a poem. The lictors waved their rods and cried out in commanding tones, "Peace! Attention!" and the eager multitude was silent.

"Friends, comrades!" began Junius, with a loud but uncertain voice —

> "Friends, comrades, since true poesy you love,
>   And bend adoringly to own its might,
> Let sadness flee, care vanish like a mist!
>   Apollo rises — conqueror of night!"

Junius had ended, and was answered on all sides by hisses, groans, and laughter.

The upturned faces of the multitude glowed with indignation; all eyes sparkled with anger; all hands were raised and threatened him with clenched fists.

"Is he turning us to ridicule?" roared angry voices. "Tear him down from the tribune, the stupid rhymester! Down with the blockhead! Pelt him with rotten apples and eggs, the fool! Stone him! Stone him!"

Junius plunged headlong from the tribune; but before he reached his house, he heard loud applause, bravas, and cries of admiration.

Tormented by doubts, Junius returned to

the public square, taking pains to pass unnoticed amid the crowd — for "fearful it is to wake the angry lion!"

And what did he see?

High upon the shoulders of the crowd, on a broad golden shield, covered with a purple mantle, his head crowned with laurels, stood his rival, the youthful poet Julius; and the crowd called out, "Honor and glory to the immortal Julius! He has consoled us in our woes, in our great sorrow! He has refreshed us with his sublime poetry, which is sweeter than honey, more fragrant than roses, more musical than cymbals, purer than the blue of the heavens. Raise him high in triumph, let soft clouds of incense rise about his inspired head, fan him with palm-leaves, strew before him all the perfumes of Arabia! Honor and glory to the divine poet!"

Junius approached one of the shouters: "Tell me, dear fellow-citizen, how ran the poem, with which Julius so pleased you. I was unfortunately away when he recited it.

Be kind enough, I beg you, to repeat it to me, if you remember it!"

"How could I forget such a verse?" was the eager answer. "What do you take me for? Hear and rejoice, make glad with all of us. The verse ran thus:—

> "'Friends, comrades, since you love true poesy,
>   And reverently adore its sacred might,
> Let care and sorrow flee before the dawn!
> Phœbus is risen — gone the clouds of night!'

"Well, what do you think of that?"

"But, if you please," exclaimed Junius, "those are my lines! Julius was among the crowd when I recited them; he heard and repeated them with a few trifling changes, which are by no means improvements!"

"Ah! now I recognize you; you are Junius!" answered the man, with a frown. "You must be either envious or a blockhead. Come to your senses, wretched man! How nobly Julius puts it,—

> "'Phœbus is risen — gone the clouds of night!'

"Just compare your stuff with that, —

"'Apollo rises — conqueror of night!'"

"Well, is not that the same thing?" began Junius.

"A word more," interrupted the citizen, "and I will call the people together, and they will tear you limb from limb."

Junius prudently held his peace. An old, gray-headed man, who had listened to the conversation, stepped up to the unhappy poet, laid his hand on his shoulder, and said:

"Junius, you recited your lines at an unfortunate time. Although Julius merely repeated the words of another, he chose the right moment to do it in; hence his success. Your own consciousness of merit must be your reward."

During the jubilee which celebrated his opponent's success, the poor, neglected Junius had nothing but his own consciousness of merit to console himself with, and, sooth to say, it consoled him ill enough.

Clad in purple and crowned with laurel, refulgent as the golden, all-conquering sun, proud, sublime, majestic, — like a king going to his coronation, — Julius strode about, surrounded by clouds of incense; palm-branches waved at his approach, and the reverence for him in the hearts of his delighted fellow-citizens knew no bounds.

APRIL, 1878.

## THE SPARROW.

I WALKED up my garden path as I was coming home from shooting. My dog ran on before me.

Suddenly he went slower, and crept carefully forward as if he scented game.

I looked along the path and perceived a young sparrow, with its downy head and yellow bill. It had fallen from a nest (the wind was blowing hard through the young birch trees beside the path), and was sprawling motionless, helpless on the ground, with its little wings outspread.

My dog crept softly up to it, when suddenly an old, black-breasted sparrow threw himself down from a neighboring tree, and let himself fall like a stone directly under the dog's nose, and, with ruffled feathers, sprang with a terrified twitter several times against his open, threatening mouth.

He had flown down to protect his young at the sacrifice of himself. His little body trembled all over, his cry was hoarse, he was frightened to death; but he sacrificed himself.

My dog must have seemed to him a gigantic monster, but for all that he could not stay on his high, safe branch. A power stronger than himself drove him down.

My dog stopped and drew back; it seemed as if he, too, respected this power.

I hastened to call back the amazed dog, and reverently withdrew. Yes,—don't laugh! I felt a reverence for this little hero of a bird, with his paternal love.

Love, thought I, is mightier than death and the fear of death; love alone inspires and is the life of all.

APRIL, 1878.

---

# THE LABORER AND THE MAN WITH THE WHITE HAND.

### A DIALOGUE.

LABORER. — What brings you here? What do you want? You don't belong to us! Go away.

THE WHITE-HANDED MAN. — I belong to you, brothers.

LABORER. — What an idea! You one of us? A likely story! Look at my hands. Don't you see how dirty they are? They smell of earth, of the barn-yard; — but look how white yours are; what do they smell of?

THE WHITE-HANDED MAN. — Here — smell!

LABORER. — What the devil is that? They seem to smell of iron!

THE WHITE-HANDED MAN. — True. I wore chains on them for six years.

LABORER. — Why?

THE WHITE-HANDED MAN. — Because I wrote in your cause; because I wished to set you poor, ignorant men free; because I strove and rebelled against your oppressors . . . that was why they put me in prison.

LABORER. — How? You've been in prison? Who told you to rebel?

### TWO YEARS LATER.

ANOTHER LABORER. — TO THE FIRST. — I say, Peter, don't you know that fellow with white hands, who came here summer before last? He talked with you.

FIRST LABORER. — Yes, — well, what about him?

SECOND LABORER. — Only think; he's going to be hung to-day! He has been condemned.

FIRST LABORER. — Has he gone on rebelling?

SECOND LABORER. — Yes, just as before!

FIRST LABORER. — Well! . . . I'll tell you what, brother Dimitry, don't you suppose we could get a bit of the rope he's hanged with? They say that such a bit of rope brings good luck to a house.

SECOND LABORER. — That is true, brother Peter. We must try.

---

## THE SKULL.

A MAGNIFICENT, brilliantly-lighted room, thronged with ladies and gentlemen.

All are talking eagerly. The conversation turns on a celebrated singer. They pronounce her divine, immortal. Oh, how charming her last trill was yesterday!

Suddenly, as if at the touch of a magician's wand, the flesh and skin vanished from all the faces and heads, and in a moment appeared the ghastly hue of the skulls, the naked gray jaw and cheek-bones.

With horror I watched the movement of those jaws and cheek-bones; I saw how the round, bony skulls shone in the lamp and candle-light, how the smaller balls of the expressionless eyes rolled about inside the larger balls of the skulls.

I dared not touch my own face or look at myself in the glass.

The skulls, however, kept on moving as before; the same gabbling was produced by the red flaps through the lifeless jaws; these nimble tongues still chattered about the astonishing last trill of the unapproachable, the immortal, yes, the *immortal* singer.

APRIL, 1878.

## THE LAST MEETING.

ONCE we were near, intimate friends . . . but the evil moment came, and we parted enemies.

Many years passed by . . . and I came to the city in which he lived, and heard that he was hopelessly ill and wished to see me.

I went to see him and entered his chamber . . . our eyes met.

I scarcely knew him. Heavens! how illness had changed him!

Yellow, wizened, not a hair on his head, with a thin, gray beard, there he sat scantily covered.

He could not bear the slightest pressure of any article of clothing. He hastily held out his horribly thin, skinny hand, and whispered with effort a few unintelligible words. Were they a welcome or a reproach?—who can tell? His emaciated breast panted heavily, and from his inflamed eyes — the pupils were contracted with pain — dropped a few slow tears.

My heart bled. . . . I sat down near him, and, involuntarily letting my eyes fall from this terrible picture of suffering, I held out my hand to him.

But it seemed to me as if it could not be his hand which clasped mine.

It seemed to me as if the tall, still, white form of a woman came between us: a long garment covered her from head to foot; her deep, dull eyes gazed into vacancy; her pale, firm lips were silent.

This woman joined our hands . . . she reconciled us forever.

Yes, Death reconciled us.

APRIL, 1878.

## THE ROSE.

It is the end of August. Autumn is just beginning.

The sun is setting. A sudden, brief shower, without thunder and lightning, had just passed over our broad plain.

The garden in front of the house glowed in the red of the sunset, and was still wet from the rain.

She was sitting by the table in the best room, and gazing thoughtfully through the half-opened door into the garden.

I knew what was passing in her soul; I knew that, after a short, painful struggle, she had given herself up for the moment to a feeling that she could no longer control.

Suddenly she rose, went swiftly out into the garden, and disappeared from view.

An hour passed — two hours; but she did not return.

Then I rose, stepped out of the house, and followed the path which I thought she had taken.

All around was dark, night had fallen. But on the damp gravel of the path could be descried, dimly visible through the darkness, a round, red object.

I stooped. It was a young half-opened rose. Two hours before I had seen this rose in her bosom.

I carefully picked the flower up from the mud, and placed it on the table by which she had been sitting.

At last she returned, and crossing the room with a light step sat down at the table.

Her face was paler than before, but more animated. She glanced quickly about in a sort of joyful confusion, with half-closed eyes, which seemed to have grown smaller.

Then she saw the rose and took it up, looked

at its crushed, soiled petals; and tears shone in her eyes.

"Why are you weeping?" I asked.

"For this rose. See what has happened to it."

Then I thought I would make a profound remark.

"Your tears will wash it clean," said I, meaningly.

"Tears do not purify, tears burn," answered she, turning away, and throwing the rose into the half-extinguished embers in the fireplace.

"Fire burns better than tears," added she, somewhat haughtily; and her beautiful eyes still met mine half-defiantly, half-joyfully.

I knew that she too had been scorched.

APRIL, 1878.

## THE VISIT.

I was sitting at the open window early in the morning of the first of May.

It was not yet dawn, there was a faint whiteness in the east; the warm, dark night was changing into the cool morning.

No mists were rising, no breath of air stirred. All was colorless, soundless . . . Yet one already felt the approach of day, and there was a strong dewy fragrance.

Suddenly a large bird flew rustling in through the open window.

I started and looked at it closely. It was no bird, but a small, winged female figure, in a long clinging garment with many folds.

It was pearl-gray all over, except that on the under side of her wings shimmered a pale pink like a half-opened rose. Her curls were confined by a garland of lilies of the valley, and two peacock feathers waved like the feelers of a butterfly above her beautifully shaped head.

She swept up and down the room a few times; her tiny face laughed, and her large clear eyes smiled and sparkled like diamonds in the enjoyment of her capricious flight.

She held in her hand the long stem of a flower of the steppes, which is called in Russia the "Czar's Sceptre," for it looks like a sceptre.

She touched my head with this flower as she flew past.

I tried to catch her . . . but she had already fluttered out of the window and disappeared.

In the garden, in the thicket of syringa bushes, the turtle-dove received her with her first coo, and the milk-white heavens became slightly tinged with rose in the direction in which she had flown.

I recognized you, goddess of fancy! You

were so kind as to pay me one last visit; and then you flew off to younger poets.

Poesy! Youth! Maidenly Beauty! Just for one moment you shone before me in the early dawn of the first day of Spring.

MAY, 1878.

———◆———

## NECESSITAS·VIS·LIBERTAS.

### A BAS-RELIEF.

A TALL, bony, old woman, with a brazen countenance and unwavering dull glance, is hastening forward with huge strides, and with her stick-like arms is pushing forward another woman.

This second woman is enormously large and strong, well-shaped, and with muscles like Hercules! Her small head is supported on a bull-like throat; she is blind, and thrusts before her a thin little girl.

This girl alone has eyes that see; she

braces herself, turns about, and raises her delicate hands; her animated face expresses impatience and determination . . . She does not wish to obey and go where they are pushing her, but is yet forced along in spite of herself.

Necessitas · Vis · Libertas.

Let him who will translate this.

MAY, 1878.

---

## THE ALMS.

In the neighborhood of a great city, along a broad highway, was walking a sick old man.

His step was wavering; his feeble feet faltered and stumbled weakly and heavily along, as if unused to walking; his clothing was ragged, his bare head drooped upon his breast. He was wholly exhausted.

He sat down on a stone by the wayside,

leaned forward, buried his face in both hands, and through his enlaced fingers tears dropped on the gray dust of the road.

He was thinking of his past.

He had once been rich and healthy;— he had ruined his health and squandered his riches on friends and enemies. And now he had not even a bit of bread. He had been deserted by all,— by his friends even sooner than by his enemies. Could he really stoop to ask for alms? His heart was filled with shame and bitterness.

And his tears kept falling and wet the gray dust.

Suddenly he heard his name called; he raised his head and saw before him a stranger, whose countenance was quiet and dignified, but not severe; his eyes were clear but not brilliant, and his glance was penetrating but not malicious.

"You have parted with all your wealth," said he, with a quiet voice. "Do you regret your generosity?"

"No, I do not regret it," answered the old man, sighing. "But now I must die."

"If there had been no poor people in the world who had stretched out their hands to you for help," continued the stranger, "then you would have had no opportunity to practise benevolence."

The old man became sunk in thought, and did not answer.

"Overcome your pride, poor man," continued the stranger. "Go and stretch out your hand and give other good men a chance to prove by their actions that they are charitable."

The old man trembled and raised his eyes . . . but the stranger had disappeared. . . . He saw a traveller in the distance.

He stepped up to him, and stretched out his hand. The traveller turned angrily away and gave him nothing.

Another came along, who gave the old man a small alms.

With this money the old man bought some

bread, and found the bread of charity tasted sweet to him. He no longer felt ashamed; on the contrary, a quiet happiness filled his soul.

MAY, 1878.

## THE INSECT.

I DREAMED that there were about twenty of us sitting by the open windows of a large room.

Women, children, and old men were to be found among us. We were all talking together on a certain familiar topic; each one spoke eagerly without listening to what the others had to say.

Suddenly a large insect, about two inches long, flew quickly into the room, circled about and settled on the wall.

It looked like a fly or wasp; the body was dirt-colored, its hard, flat wings were of the same color; it had claw-like, hairy feet, and a large, square head like a dragon-fly. Its head and feet were blood-red.

This strange insect kept stretching its head up and down, to the right and to the left, and moving its feet at the same time . . . Then it left the wall, and flew noiselessly about in the chamber, lighted somewhere else, and began stretching itself in the same disgusting way as before.

It inspired us all with loathing, fright, even horror. . . . No one had ever seen anything like it before, and all exclaimed: "Drive out the terrible thing!" and shook their handkerchiefs at it; but no one dared to go near it . . . and all shrank away involuntarily when it flew in their direction.

But one among us, a pale young man, looked at the rest of us with astonishment. He shrugged his shoulders, smiled, and could not at all understand what was the matter with us all, and what we were so excited about. He neither saw the insect nor heard the ominous rustling of its wings.

Suddenly the insect seemed to see him. It flew up above him, then settling slowly down on to his head, it stung him on the forehead. The young man gave a slight cry, and fell dead.

The terrible fly flew away . . . and then we first guessed what sort of a visitor we had had.

MAY, 1878.

———◆———

## THE CABBAGE-SOUP.

THE only son of a widowed peasant woman had died. He was a young man of twenty, the best workman in the village.

The lady of the village heard of the woman's loss, and went to see her on the day of the funeral.

She found her at home. Standing before a table in the middle of the hut, she was steadily ladling up cabbage-soup from an earthen vessel, and slowly swallowing it down spoonful after spoonful.

The old woman's face was sad and troubled, her eyes red and swollen . . . but in spite of this she was standing there as erect and firm as if she were in church.

Heavens! thought the lady. . . . Can she eat at such a moment? . . . How little feeling these people have!

And the lady now remembered how, when she had lost her little nine-year old daughter some years before, she had been so overcome with grief as not to care to hire a beautiful villa in the neighborhood of Petersburg, but had spent the whole summer in the city! But this woman went on eating cabbage-soup.

At length the lady grew impatient, and said: "In Heaven's name! Tatiana, I am surprised. . . . Did not you love your son at all? Is it possible that you have not lost your appetite? How can you eat cabbage-soup at such a time?"

"My Wassia is dead," said the woman,

softly, and the tears ran down her hollow cheeks; "I shall soon die too! My head has been cut off while I was yet living! . . . But why should the soup be wasted? It has been salted."

The lady merely shrugged her shoulders and went away. Salt costs her nothing.

MAY, 1878.

———♦———

## THE HAPPY LAND.

O HAPPY land! O land of bliss, of light, of youth, of joy! I have seen you in my dreams. We found ourselves on a beautiful, gayly decorated boat. The sail swelled out like a swan's breast beneath the gay pennants.

My companions were unknown to me; but I felt with my whole being that they were as young, gay, and happy as I.

I scarcely regarded them, but only gazed around me over the boundless blue sea with its shining waves of gold; over my head was just such another boundless blue sea, and over it glided, smiling and gay, the bright sun on its circuitous course.

Now and then there arose from among us loud, joyous laughter, like the laughter of the gods.

Sometimes words escaped from our lips, verses of heavenly beauty, inspiration, and power. . . . The heaven itself seemed to echo in answer, and the ocean around quivered with sympathy. Then came blissful quiet.

Lightly dipping in the gentle waves swam the swift boat, not moved by the winds, but governed by the beating of our own hearts. Obedient to our wishes, it glided along like a living thing.

We met with some islands on our course,—enchanted islands, beaming with all the colors of the richest jewels, rubies, emeralds. Intoxicating perfumes rose from their curving shores. One of these islands showered us with roses and lilies of the valley; from another long-winged, rainbow-feathered birds arose.

The birds flew in wide circles over our heads, the may-bells and roses sank into the pearly foam which glided past the slippery sides of our boat.

Sweet, enticing sounds meet us together with the flowers and birds . . . bewitching womanly voices resounded; and all about, sky and sea, the waving of the well-filled sail, the murmur of the waves at the prow, all sang of love, happy, blissful love.

And the beloved one of each of us was there . . . invisible yet near. Yet a moment, and her eyes beam upon you, that is, her smile. Her hand clasps yours, and leads you into an eternal Paradise.

O Land of Happiness! I saw you in a dream.

JUNE, 1878.

## WHO IS THE RICHER?

IF they praise in my presence the rich Rothschild, who gives from his thousands towards the education of poor children, the healing of the sick, and the care of the aged, I am touched and praise him.

But while I am touched and praise him, I involuntarily remember a wretched, poverty-stricken peasant family who received a poor orphan, a relation of theirs, into their miserable, tumble-down hut.

"We will take Katey in," said the wife, — "it will cost us our last penny; we shan't be able even to afford salt to salt our soup with."

"Well, then, we will eat it unsalted," answered the peasant, her husband.

Rothschild does not compare with this peasant!

JULY, 1878.

## THE OLD MAN.

Dark, gloomy days came,—his own illness, the misfortune of those dear to him, the coldness and darkness of old age. All that thou didst love, all that was dear and precious to thee, all has passed away and fallen in ruins. Thou art on the downward path.

But what can one do? Complain? Lament? That does no one any good.

An old dying tree has fewer and smaller leaves, but yet has some green.

Withdraw into thyself, take refuge in thine own heart, live in thy recollections. There, in the depths of thy soul, will all thine early life, as thou alone knowest it, rise anew before thee with all the sweet, vivid freshness and force and charm of the spring.

But, poor old man, don't look towards the future!

July, 1878.

## THE NEWSPAPER CORRESPONDENT.

Two friends are sitting at table and drinking tea.

Suddenly there is heard a noise in the street, — railing, groaning, jeering, laughter.

"Some one is getting a beating!" remarked one of the friends, looking out.

"A criminal? . . . Perhaps a murderer?" shouted the other. "Listen! Whoever it may be, such high-handed proceedings should not be allowed. Come, let us go and help him."

"It is no murderer whom they are beating."

"No murderer? A thief, then! All right; come, let's free him from the hands of the mob."

"It's no thief, either."

"What! not a thief? Then it must be a cashier, a railroad constructor, an army contractor, a Russian Mecænas, a lawyer, a well-meaning newspaper editor, a public benefactor. It makes no difference; let us go and help him."

"No, it is a newspaper correspondent whom they are beating."

"Oh! is it? A newspaper correspondent! Well — do you know — I think we had better finish our tea first."

JULY, 1878.

## TWO BROTHERS.

I HAD a vision.

Two angels appeared to me, two genii.

I call them genii, — for both were naked, and had long, strong wings on their shoulders.

Both were youths. One was well-built, with glossy black curls. He had fiery brown eyes with thick eye-lashes; his expression was attractive, cheerful, and eager; his face was charming, fascinating, somewhat bold and saucy-looking. The full rosy lips twitched occasionally. The youth smiled like a conqueror, self-consciously and indolently; a splendid garland of flowers rested on his glossy curls, and almost touched his velvety eye-brows. A spotted leopard-skin, fastened with a golden arrow, hung easily from his plump shoulders down over his rounded hips. The feathers of his wings had a reddish shimmer, and were tipped with bright red, as if just dipped in fresh crimson blood. From time to time these wings shivered with a silvery sound like the rustling of spring rain.

The other is pale and sallow. His ribs stick out at every breath. His hair is thin, light, and smooth. His eyes are large, round, and light gray, with a strikingly clear, restless glance. All his features are sharp; his small, half-opened mouth has pointed teeth like fishes' teeth. He has a small, aquiline nose, and his prominent chin is covered with light down. His thin lips have never once smiled.

It is a regular, fear-inspiring, unsympathetic face. (The other one's face, too, although sweet and lovely to look at, expresses no sympathy.) The head of the second is hung about with scanty, empty ears of corn, bound with withered grasses. A rough gray garment covers his loins; his wings, which are of a dull dark blue, move slowly and threateningly.

The youths seem inseparable companions. Each of them leans on the shoulder of the other. The soft hand of the first lies like a full bunch of grapes on the other's bony shoulder, while the second one's hand with its long, snake-like fingers rests on the rounder breast of the other. . . . And I heard a voice which said: —

"Love and Hunger — two brothers, the foundation pillars of all life, stand before you.

"Every living thing struggles to feed itself, and feeds itself in order to reproduce itself.

"Love and Hunger — their aim is the same, — preservation of life, of one's own life and the life of others, — the life of all."

August, 1878.

---

## IN MEMORY OF I. P. W.

On dirty, damp, rotten straw, in the garret of an old house, which had been hastily converted into a field-hospital, in a deserted Bulgarian village, — she lay dying of typhus for two long weeks.

She had become unconscious, and the surgeons troubled themselves no longer about her; but the sick soldiers, whom she had tended as long as she could keep on her feet, took turns in rising from their sick-beds to moisten her parched lips with a few drops of water.

She was young and beautiful, known to the upper ranks of society, and high dignitaries had paid her attention. She was envied by ladies and courted by gentlemen. . . . Two or three men had loved her warmly and silently. Life smiled upon her; but there are some smiles that are worse than tears.

Such a gentle, loving heart, — and such strength, such self-sacrifice! She knew no other happiness than to help the needy; she knew no other, and learnt to know no other. Every other joy passed by her unheeded. She had long become reconciled to this. Her whole being was filled with the warmth of an inextinguishable faith, and her life was wholly devoted to the service of her fellow-creatures.

What imperishable treasures lay buried in the depths and secret places of her soul, no one knew; and now no one will ever know.

And why should they? . . . The sacrifice is complete . . . her work is done.

But it is a sad thought that her body received no single word of thanks, although she modestly shunned all thanks.

May her lovely shadow not be annoyed by this tardy blossom, which I venture to place upon her grave.

SEPTEMBER, 1878.

---

## THE EGOTIST.

HE had all the qualities best calculated to make him a scourge to his family.

He had been rich and healthy from his birth, and rich and healthy he remained his whole life through. He never allowed himself to be led astray, he had no failings, never made a promise that he was not both able and willing to keep, and never failed in what he undertook.

His honesty was unimpeachable, and he oppressed every one — relations, friends, acquaintances — with his proud consciousness of this honesty.

His honesty was his capital, for which he drew high interest. His honesty gave him the right to be pitiless, and to refuse all favors not prescribed by law. He stood on his rights without pity or kindness; for kindness, performed by rule, is no kindness.

He never looked out for any one except for his own exemplary self, and he was extremely exasperated if others did not take all care of his own estimable personality.

With all this, he did not at all consider himself an egotist; on the contrary, he was very severe in his blame of egotism and egotists — naturally! the egotism of others interfered with his own egotism.

As he was conscious of having no weak points himself, he neither understood nor excused weakness in others. In point of fact, he understood no one and nothing; for he was entirely, on all sides, above and below, before and behind, hemmed in and surrounded by self.

He had no comprehension of what forgiveness meant. He had never had occasion to pardon anything in himself. How could he know how to forgive others?

This monster of virtue raised his eyes to the face of his God, before the bar of his own conscience, and said with firm clear voice, "Yes, I am a good, virtuous man."

Even on his deathbed will he repeat these words, and feel no emotion in his heart of stone, — in his spotless, perfect heart.

Oh! the ugliness of self-satisfied, rigid, cheap virtue, almost more loathsome than the naked ugliness of vice.

DECEMBER, 1878.

## THE SUPREME BEING'S BANQUET.

It once occurred to the Supreme Being to give a banquet in his azure halls.

All the virtues were invited to it,—none but the virtues, ... so there were no men— only women.

Many of these were assembled there, great and small. The smaller virtues were more agreeable and amiable than the great; but all seemed in good spirits, and conversed very politely with one another, as beseemed such near relations and acquaintances.

Then the Supreme Being noticed two beautiful ladies, who did not seem to know each other.

The host took one lady by the hand and led her up to the other.

"Benevolence!" said he, pointing to the first.

"Gratitude!" added he, introducing the second to her.

Both virtues were much surprised to make each other's acquaintance. For the first time since the creation of the world, and that was a great while ago, they now met face to face.

DECEMBER, 1878.

## THE NYMPHS.

I WAS standing before a splendid, crescent-shaped extended chain of mountains, which were covered from top to bottom by a green young wood.

The transparent blue of the southern sky was above them, the sunbeams were playing on their summits. Swift-running brooks, half concealed in verdure, were murmuring below.

Then I remembered the old story of the Greek ship, which in the first century after the birth of Christ sailed the Ægean sea:—

It was high noon and the weather was calm. Suddenly a voice sounded from above, over the head of the steersman: "When you pass by the island, call with a loud voice, 'Great Pan is dead!'" The steersman was astonished and frightened. But when the ship came by the island, he obeyed and called out, "Great Pan is dead!" And at once were heard, as if in answer to his call, all along the shore of this uninhabited island, loud sobbing, groaning, and moaning cries: "He is dead, dead; great Pan is dead."

I was thinking of this legend, and a sudden thought occurred to me. What if I too were to call out something?

But in the presence of all the loveliness around, I could not think of death. I called with all my might:—"He has risen; great Pan has risen!"

And suddenly, a miracle! There echoed immediately as if in answer to my call, along the whole broad crescent of the green mountains, a universal laugh and murmur and joyous prattling. "He has risen; Pan has risen!" cried youthful voices. All around me broke out gay rejoicing, brighter than the sun overhead, gayer than the brooks running under the grass. Hasty steps approached; through the green thicket shimmered alabaster white garments and rosy bare limbs. They were the nymphs! nymphs, dryads, bacchantes, who hastened down from the heights into the valleys.

All along the glades they suddenly appeared, their godlike heads adorned with clustering curls; garlands and tambourines in their hands; laughter, ringing Olympian laughter, echoed and rolled down before them.

First of all advances the goddess; she is the stateliest, most beautiful of all — with her quiver on her shoulder, her bow in her hand, and the silver crescent moon on her curls.

Diana! — is it thou?

But suddenly the goddess stops, motionless. The nymphs follow her example. The clear laughter dies away. In indescribable terror, with parted lips, she gazes with startled eyes into the distance.

I turned to follow the direction of her gaze. Across the fields, on the uttermost limit of the horizon, shone like a fiery point the golden cross on the white steeple of a Christian church. The goddess had seen this cross.

I heard behind me a long trembling sigh, like the trembling of a broken harp-string, and when I again looked round, the nymphs had vanished. The broad forest shone green as before, and here and there, through the thick tangle of the branches, shimmered and faded a gleam of white. Was it the garments of the nymphs or the rising mist from the valley, — I know not.

Yet how sorry I was for the vanished goddess.

**December, 1878.**

## THE SPHINX.

Yellowish, gray, creaking sand, loose on the surface, but firm underneath. . . . Sand without end, wherever one looks.

And over this sandy desert, over this sea of dead dust, arises the gigantic head of a sphinx.

What do these thick, projecting lips wish to say?—these broad, spreading nostrils, and these eyes, these long, half-sleepy, half-observant eyes, under the double curve of their high brows?

They have indeed something to say! They even say it; but Œdipus alone can solve the riddle, and understand its dumb speech.

Ah! . . . I recognize these features. They have no longer anything Egyptian about them. The low white brow, the prominent cheek-bones, the short straight nose, the pretty mouthful of white teeth, the soft moustache, and the curly beard on the chin. . . . And these small eyes set wide apart, this thick hair in the form of a cap, and parted in the middle. . . . There you are, Karp, Sidor, Simon!

Little peasant from Jaroslaw, Riazan — you, my countryman . . . when did you turn sphinx?

Or have you really anything to say? Yes, you too are indeed a sphinx.

Your eyes, those colorless but deep eyes, also speak, . . . and their expression, too, is dumb and enigmatic.

But where is your Œdipus?

Ah, it is not enough to put on the cap of a Slavophile to be your Œdipus, — oh, you old Russian Sphinx!

DECEMBER, 1878.

# THE FRIEND AND THE ENEMY.

A PRISONER condemned to lifelong confinement escaped from his prison and took flight.

His pursuers were on his heels.

He ran with all speed and outstripped them.

Suddenly he saw before him the steep bank of a river, a narrow but deep river. He could not swim.

One single rotten plank bridged it. The fugitive had already his foot upon it. . . . His best friend and his worst enemy happened to be there on the shore.

His enemy folded his arms, but said nothing; the friend, on the other hand, called out, "For Heaven's sake! what are you doing? Don't you see that the board is rotten? It will break under your weight, and you will certainly drown!"

"But there is no other way of getting across! . . . and my pursuers . . . don't you hear them?" groaned the wretched man despairingly, and stepped upon the plank.

"I will not let you! No, you shall not go to your ruin!" exclaimed the zealous friend, pulling the board away from under the feet of the fugitive, who was hurled into the rushing waves and drowned.

The enemy laughed complacently and went away; but the friend sat down on the shore and wept bitterly for his poor, poor friend.

It did not occur to him for a moment that he could be to blame for his death.

"He would not take my advice! He would not take my advice," he whispered sadly.

"At any rate," said he at last, "he would have been forced to languish his whole life long in that frightful prison. Now he is freed from his sufferings! It is easier for him so. It was his fate.

"But, humanly speaking, I am sorry all the same!"

And the good soul sobbed, and was long inconsolable over his friend's unhappy fate.

DECEMBER, 1878.

---

## CHRIST.

ONCE when I was a lad, scarcely more than a boy, I happened to be in a lovely village church. The thin wax candles glowed like red points before the pictures of the saints.

A rainbow-colored glow surrounded each flame. It was dim and dark in the church, but many people were there standing in front of me.

They were all brown-haired peasants' heads, which moved up and down in a wave-like motion, rising and falling like ripe ears of wheat when tossing in the summer wind.

Suddenly some one stepped in behind me, and placed himself near me.

I did not turn, but had nevertheless a feeling that this man — was Christ.

I was overcome by emotion, curiosity, and fright all at once. I controlled myself, and looked at my neighbors.

He had a countenance like other people's; — a countenance like any other man's face. The eyes were looking softly and attentively upward. The lips were closed, but not compressed; the upper lip seemed to rest on the lower. His beard was not long and was parted at the chin. His hands were folded and motionless. Even his dress was like that of others.

Can this be Christ? I thought, — such an unpretending, perfectly simple person? It is not possible.

I turned away, but, scarcely had I withdrawn my glance from this plain man, when it seemed to me that he who was standing by me must really be Christ.

I looked at him once more, and again I saw the same face that looked like the faces of all other men; the same every-day though unfamiliar features.

At last I became uncomfortable, and collected myself. Then it suddenly became clear to me that Christ had really just such a common human face.

June, 1878.

———◆———

## THE STONE.

Have you ever seen an old gray stone lying on the shore of the ocean, where at high-tide on a sunny day the pulsing waves wash up around it, fawn upon it, caressingly embrace it, and sprinkle its mossy bed with a plashing, pearly shower?

The stone remains always the same, though its dark surface shines in brighter colors.

These colors bear witness that once long ago, when the liquid granite had scarcely begun to cool, it glowed through and through with fiery tints.

So was it too with my old heart, when a short time since young womanly beings laid siege to it from all sides;—beneath their caressing touch the long-faded tints revived and shone with their former glow.

The waves have ebbed . . . but the colors have not wholly disappeared, although a sharp wind is effacing them more and more.

MAY, 1879.

———◆———

## THE DOVES.

I STOOD on the top of a softly-swelling hill; before me lay a field of rye, like an ocean bright with silver and gold. There was no motion of waves on this sea; the sultry air was unstirred,—a mighty thunder-storm was approaching.

Where I was the sun still shone warm; but yonder, over the other side of the field, not very far off, hung a dark-blue thunder-cloud, like a monstrous burden over half the vault of heaven.

Everything sought shelter . . . everything groaned beneath the ominous glow of the last sunbeams. There was no bird in sight, none uttered a note; even the sparrow had crept away and hidden itself.

How strong was the perfume of the wormwood in the grove! I looked up at the dark thunder-cloud, . . . and a feeling of unrest took possession of my spirit. Now then quick, quick! I thought. Gleam, golden serpent; thunder, roll! Come up here, come on; fling down your masses of water, grim clouds! Shorten this terrible waiting!

Yet the storm-cloud stirred not. It only weighed down as oppressively as ever upon the silent earth, and seemed to pile itself ever higher and grow yet darker.

Suddenly an object shone out, floating lightly against the monotonous dark background of the cloud. It looked like a white handkerchief or like a snow-ball;—it was a white dove flying over from the village.

It flew and flew always straight ahead . . . at last it disappeared behind the wood.

A few moments went by; the same oppressive quiet still reigned. But look! Now there are two little handkerchiefs, two snowballs, shining there and flying back, two white doves taking their quiet flight homewards.

And now at last the storm broke loose, and the dance began!

I had scarcely time to reach the house. The wind whistled and roared mightily; low, tawny, ragged clouds scurried by. All whirled dizzily in mad confusion together: the mighty pouring rain beat and rattled down in vertical streams; the lightning flashed its blinding, greenish fire; there was a smell of brimstone.

Under an overhanging roof, on the very edge of the dormer window, sit two white doves side by side, — the one who flew out to fetch his companion, and the other who was perhaps saved by him.

Both are smoothing their feathers and pressing close together.

They are happy! and while I watch them I am happy, although I am alone, — alone as always.

MAY, 1879.

———◆———

## TO-MORROW, TO-MORROW!

How empty and dull, how insignificant is almost every day that passes by me! How few traces each one leaves behind it! How meaningless are all these hours that pass one after the other!

And yet, in spite of all, man wishes to live; he values life, he hopes for something from it, from himself, from the future. . . . Oh, what a rich blessing he expects from the future!

But why does he imagine that future days will not be like the past?

He does not imagine it. He does not like to think much about it; and there he is right.

"Well, to-morrow, to-morrow!" He comforts himself with this "to-morrow" until it finally leads him to the grave.

And when one is once in one's grave — then thought ceases of itself.

MAY, 1879.

## NATURE.

ONCE I dreamed that I was in a great subterranean, high-arched hall. The whole hall was lit up by an equal light, which seemed to come from beneath the earth.

In the middle of this hall sat the majestic form of a woman, clothed in a loose green dress. With her head supported in her hand, she seemed sunk in profound thought.

I soon guessed that this woman must be Nature herself; and a reverential fear, like a sudden shiver, penetrated my soul.

I approached her, and greeting her respectfully, I cried: "O, Mother of us all! on what are you meditating? Are you perhaps thinking of the future fate of mankind, or of the long road that man must travel in order to reach the greatest possible perfection — the highest happiness?"

The woman slowly turned her dark, terrible eyes, her lips moved, and with a thundering metallic voice she spoke:—

"I am considering how to give greater strength to the muscles in a flea's, leg so that it may escape more easily from its enemies. The equilibrium between attack and defence is lost, and must be restored."

"Wh-a-t?" stammered I, "is that what you are thinking about? Are not we men then your dearest, favorite children?"

The woman frowned slightly, and said: "All creatures are my children; I care equally for you all, — and annihilate all without distinction."

"But virtue — reason — justice?" I stammered again.

"Those are human words!" resounded the

brazen voice, "I recognize no good or bad; reason is no law for me; and what is justice? I gave you life; I take it from you and give it to others, — worms or men, it is all the same to me . . . but as for thee, protect thyself for a while, and leave me in peace."

I strove to answer, but the earth groaned and trembled, and I awoke.

AUGUST, 1879.

---

## "HANG HIM!"

IT was in the year 1803, began my old friend, not very long before Austerlitz. The regiment in which I was an officer was stationed in Moravia.

We were strictly forbidden to molest or oppress the inhabitants; nevertheless we were looked upon with suspicion, although we were allies.

I had for body-servant a fellow called Jegor, a former serf of my mother's. He was an honest, quiet fellow. I had known him all his life, and treated him like a friend.

Now, one day there arose outcries and complaints in the house in which I lodged. Some one had stolen two hens from the woman of the house, and she accused my servant of the theft. He sought to defend himself and called me to witness. . . . He, Jegor Avtamonov, a thief? I assured the woman that he was honest, but she would not listen to me.

Suddenly there was a tramp of horses in the street. It was the Commander-in-chief, who was passing with his staff.

He was riding by at a walk; a stout, thick-set man, with his head bent and his epaulettes hanging forward on his chest.

When the woman saw him she threw herself, with dishevelled hair, on her knees before his horse, seized his stirrup, and complained loudly of my man, whom she pointed out.

"General!" cried she, "your Honor!

Judge us! Defend us! Save us! This soldier has robbed me."

Jegor stood on the threshold of the house as straight as a ramrod, his chest out, his heels together, his cap in his hand; but he uttered not a word.

Whether Jegor was overawed by the sight of all these generals who had stopped before him in the middle of the street, or whether he was petrified at the thought of his impending danger, I do not know: he stood stiffly there, casting down his eyes, and as pale as a sheet.

The Commander-in-chief glanced carelessly and frowningly at him, and growled out, "Well?" Jegor stood there stiff and motionless, showing his teeth like an idiot; one might almost have thought he was laughing.

Then said the Commander-in-chief abruptly, "Hang him!" He spurred his horse and rode on, first at a walk, then at a gentle trot, followed by his whole staff. Only one adjutant turned in his saddle and glanced for an instant at Jegor.

It was impossible to disregard such a command; Jegor was seized and led off to execution.

Then for the first time he shrank from death, and called out earnestly once or twice: "Lord God, help me!" and added, under his breath, "As God is my witness, I did not do it!"

He wept bitterly on taking leave of me. I was in despair. "Jegor, Jegor!" I exclaimed, "why did n't you speak to the general?"

"As God is my witness, it was not I who did it," repeated the poor fellow, sobbing. Even the woman herself was horrified. She had not at all expected such a fearful result, and she, on her part, began to cry and shriek; wringing her hands, she begged each and every one to have mercy, that she had found her hens, that she would explain everything.

Of course all this led to no result. That is

the way of war, my dear sir, — military discipline! The woman sobbed terribly.

Jegor, who had already confessed to the priest and partaken of the last communion, turned to me: "Tell her, sir, that she must not grieve so. I have already forgiven her."

My friend, when he had repeated these last words of his servant, whispered, "My little Jegor, my dear fellow, you good lad!" and the tears ran down his cheeks.

AUGUST, 1879.

---

## WHAT SHALL I THINK ABOUT?

WHAT shall I think about, when I am dying, — provided that I am in a condition to think at all?

Shall I think I have made a poor use of my life? That I have idled and dreamed it away? That I have not known how to make the most of its gifts?

What? Has death come already? So soon?

Impossible!... I have really not had time to do anything! I was just going to undertake...

Shall I think of the past? Will my thoughts be directed to the few bright moments I have had — to beloved forms and persons?

---

## "HOW LOVELY AND FRESH THOSE ROSES WERE!"

SOMEWHERE, sometime, long, long ago, I read a poem, which I soon forgot. Only the first line remained in my memory, —

" How lovely and fresh those roses were!"

Now it is winter; the window-panes are covered with frost; a single lamp burns in the dim chamber. I sit in the corner, and there keeps running in my head,

" How lovely and fresh those roses were!"

I see myself before the low window of a Russian country-house. The summer day is sinking gently to rest and passing into night; the soft air is filled with the fragrance of mignonette and of the blooming lindens. On the window-seat is sitting a girl supported by her upraised arm, her head bending toward her shoulder. She is gazing fixedly and silently up into the sky as if watching for the stars to come out. How full of feeling are those dreamy eyes; how touchingly innocent her half-opened, questioning lips; how quietly rises and falls her girlish bosom as yet undisturbed by passion; and how pure and tender is the outline of her youthful face! I do not venture to address her; but how dear she is to me, how my heart beats!

"How lovely and fresh those roses were!"

In the room it grows ever darker . . . the lamp which has burnt low flickers, and fugitive shadows tremble on the low ceiling. The sharp frost creaks loudly outside the wall, and I hear nothing but the sad whisper of old age:—

"How lovely and fresh those roses were!"

Other scenes from the past arise before me. I hear the joyous bustle of family life. Two little brown curly heads, pressed one against the other, look me in the face with their roguish eyes; their rosy cheeks dimple with suppressed laughter; their hands are clasped lovingly together; the caressing youthful voices mingle joyously, and in the background of the cosy old room young uncertain fingers wander over the keys of a worn-out old pianoforte, and do not succeed in drowning the humming of the samovar in the notes of the Lanner *valse!*

"How lovely and fresh those roses were!"

... The lamp goes out and it is dark. Who is that coughing there so hoarsely? Rolled up at my feet lies my only companion, the old dog, shivering and starting in his sleep. I am cold . . . all, all are dead, . . . all dead!

"How lovely and fresh those roses were!"

SEPTEMBER, 1879.

## A TRIP BY SEA.

I CROSSED in a little steamer from Hamburg to London. There were two of us passengers, — I and a little ape, a little female *uistiti*, which a Hamburg merchant was sending as a present to his English partner.

The little animal was fastened by a slender chain to a bench on the deck, and it twitched at its chain and peeped complainingly like a bird.

Every time I passed, it stretched out to me its cold black hand, and looked fixedly at me with its sad, almost human, eyes. I took its hand, and it stopped peeping and twitching.

There came a calm. The sea lay before us like a motionless leaden sheet. It did not seem vast; for it was hemmed in by a thick fog, which even hid the top of the masts and wearied our eyes by its impenetrability. The sun hung like a dull red spot in the dark mist; but toward evening it brightened and spread over the heaven a mysterious, ominous, red glow.

Long straight folds, like folds of heavy silk, extended downward from the prow and spread apart, curled up, and smoothed themselves out again, at last disappearing in ripples. The whirling foam bubbled up like milk beneath the monotonously plunging wheels, spreading apart, then flowing together in snake-like jets, again to disappear and be swallowed up by the thick fog.

The ding-dong of the little bell at the stern sounded carelessly and complainingly; it was as wearing as the squeaking of the ape.

Here and there arose a seal, but to disappear again, plunging headlong under the slightly rippled surface.

The captain, a silent man, with a dark sun-burnt face, smoked his short pipe, and spat moodily into the motionless sea.

He only answered my questions by a short

growl, so that I was, in spite of myself, thrown for companionship on my only fellow-voyager, the ape.

I sat down by it, it ceased its peeping, and again held its hand out to me.

The perpetual fog veiled us in its dreamy circle of mist. We sat side by side like two relations, alike in unconscious meditation.

Now, I smile at this . . . then, I felt differently.

We are all the children of one mother; and it was pleasant to me to see the poor little animal grow trustfully quiet, and lean up against me like a friend.

NOVEMBER, 1879.

## N. N.

HARMONIOUSLY and quietly, without tears as without smiles, you pass through life, unattached by the commonest ties.

You are good and wise . . . but you are remote from all, and depend on none.

You are beautiful, and no one can accuse you of setting any store by your beauty. You are unsympathetic yourself, and you ask for nobody's sympathy.

Your eyes are deep but not meditative; in their clear depth is emptiness.

Such harmonious shadows as you wander in the Elysian fields to the sublime notes of Gluck's melodies, joyless and sorrowless.

NOVEMBER, 1879.

## STOP!

Stop! As I see you now, remain forever in my memory. From your lips has escaped the last inspired tone. Your glance does not beam and sparkle; it is dim, overcome by the blessed consciousness of that beauty which it has been given to you to express . . . of that beauty towards which you seem to hold out triumphant yet weary arms.

What a gleam — tenderer and purer than the light of the sun — lights up your whole form, even the least fold of your garments!

What god's caressing breath has thrown back your loose curls?

His kisses burn yet on your white alabaster brow. See, there is manifest the mystery of poetry, of life, of love! See immortality there! There is no need of any other. For this moment you are immortal! This moment will pass away, and you will become again a pinch of ashes, a woman, a child. . . . But what matters it to you? For this one moment you are higher, more sublime than all things mortal, changeable. For this moment you are immortal.

Stop, and let me share your immortality; let fall into my soul a beam of your eternal beauty!

NOVEMBER, 1879.

## THE MONK.

I KNEW a monk,—a hermit, a holy man. He lived only for the delights of prayer, and, intoxicated by it, he would stand so long on the cold floor of the church that his legs would swell from the knees downward, and become like stone pillars. They lost all feeling, while he stood there and prayed.

I understood him,—even envied, him perhaps; but he ought to understand me too, and not despise one to whom his joys are unattainable.

He has succeeded in annihilating his hated self; but if I cannot pray, it is not from egotism!

My self is perhaps more burdensome and hateful to me than his to him.

He has found a means of forgetting himself; but I too find forgetfulness of self sometimes, if not always.

He is no hypocrite — but neither am I.

NOVEMBER, 1879.

---

## LET'S KEEP A GOOD HEART.

WHAT an unimportant trifle may often change the course of a man's life!

Once I was going thoughtfully along the highway.

My soul was weighed down by heavy forebodings. I was overcome with despondency.

I raised my head . . . straight before me ran the road between two stiff rows of poplars. And across the road, about ten paces in front of me, were hopping in single file a family of sparrows, full of life, merriment and courage.

One, in particular, distinguished himself by his bold, sideways hopping; he stuck out his little breast, and twittered as bravely as if he did not fear the devil himself. A true conqueror!

Meanwhile, a hawk circled overhead, whose destiny it was, perhaps, to devour this very hero.

I looked, was forced to laugh, and regained my self-possession. My gloomy thoughts had vanished; I felt again courage, energy, and life.

A hawk may be circling over me; but the devil take it!— let's keep a good heart!

November, 1879.

## PRAYER.

Whatever a man may pray for, he prays for a miracle. Every prayer comes to this: "Great God, let twice two not make four."

Only such a prayer is a real prayer, face to face. To pray to the Spirit of the universe, to the Supreme Being, — to the abstract, unreal god of Kant or Hegel, — is impossible, unthinkable.

But can a personal, living, imaginable God make twice two other than four?

Every true believer must answer, "Yes. He can." And he is obliged to convince himself of it.

But what if his reason rebels against such nonsense?

Then Shakspere comes to his aid: "There are more things in heaven and earth, Horatio."

But if you seek to controvert him in the

name of truth? He has merely to repeat the well-known question, "What is truth?"

And so, let us eat, drink, and be merry,— and pray.

July, 1881

## THE RUSSIAN LANGUAGE.

In these days of doubt, in these days of painful brooding over the fate of my country, you alone are my rod and my staff, O great, mighty, true, and free Russian language! If it were not for you, how could one keep from despairing at the sight of what is going on at home? But it is inconceivable that such a language should not belong to a great people.

June, 1882.

# THE CATALOGUE

OF THE

# ART DEPARTMENT

OF THE

## MANUFACTURERS AND MECHANICS INSTITUTE,

### BOSTON, MASS.

### ❧ 1883 ❧

Is the most magnificent effort yet made in this country to place before the public, in a single, compact volume, the results that to this date have been reached in American Art. It excels all catalogues of Art that have been produced either in this country or in Europe, and is designed to serve many other purposes than the one that was the immediate occasion of its production. It was planned and executed with immense pains, and absolutely regardless of cost, by John M. Little, the Chairman, and Frank T. Robinson, the Art Director, of the Exposition, solely in the interests of the Art and the Art-Industries of this country. One motive pervades the whole book, and finds enthusiastic expression in its every page; namely, to produce a work which for practical value and importance should be attractive alike to artists, designers, photographers, printers, manufacturers, indeed to all whose professions and livelihoods are allied with Art and Art-progress.

It is a large quarto of 300 pages, printed at the Art Age Press of Arthur B. Turnure, New York, who has succeeded in making it, in point of paper, printing, and style, an ideal instance of the typography and bibliopegy of the nineteenth century. It contains 63 full-page illustrations, all of which have been judiciously selected from the most notable works of the best American artists; and, as produced here, are intended to show the facilities possessed of artistic illustration and the effectiveness of reproductive methods in the Art-world.

## ORIGINAL ETCHINGS

Of surpassing beauty have been contributed by the following distinguished artists, as well as by others:—

Stephen Parish,
Thomas Moran,
C. A. Platt,
Charles Volkmar,
B. Lander,

J. C. Nicoll,
A. H. Bicknell,
R. C. Miner,

C. H. Ritchie,
William Hart,
J. A. S. Monks,
George L. Brown,
W. F. Lansil.

## FULL-PAGE DRAWINGS

Appear by these, among other well-known names:—

| | | |
|---|---|---|
| Carroll Beckwith, | Carl Chapman, | J. Wagner, |
| R. Bunner, | R. H. Burleigh, | C. W. Sanderson, |
| Thomas Robinson, | F. Batchellor, | E. M. Parmenter, |
| C. D. Hunt, | W. A. Coffin, | Leo Hunter, |
| Bruce Crane, | F. Childe Hassam, | T. Winthrop Pierce, |
| E. H. Blashfield, | F. M. Boggs, | Julia Dabney, |
| R. W. Van Boskerck, | Granville Perkins, | H. M. Knowlton, |
| R. M. Shurtleff, | | Eleanor Matlock. |

All persons interested in the historical development, present position, and the prospects of the young American Art School, will find unusually instructive and opportune the series of papers contributed by the ablest living specialists in knowledge of the theories and practice of Art; which considered in their entirety may be said to constitute a literature on Modern Art and Modern Art-tendencies.

The quality and interest of the text is seen from a glance at the

## SUBJECTS AND CONTRIBUTORS:

*Photography*, Edward A. Robinson.
*American Art Furniture*, A. Curtis Bond.
*The Growth of American Art*, James Jackson Jarves.
*Journalism and Art*, M. G. Van Rensselaer.
*Portrait Painting*, Sidney Dickenson.
*Native Painters*, Charles DeKay.
*American Flower Painters*, C. Wheeler.
*Etchings*, S. R. Koehler.
*Landscape Art*, William Howe Downes.
*Watercolor Painting*, Lyman H. Weeks.
*American Wood Engraving*, Arlo Bates.
*Color in Works of Art*, R. Riordan.
*The Ideal in American Art*, Florence Finch.
*American Art Journalism*, James B. Townsend.
*Success in Art*, F. T. Lent.
*The Art Tariff*, L. C. Knight.
*Memorial Art*, E. H. Silsbee.
*What shall American Artists Paint?* E. H. Clement.
*The Present Conditions of American Art*, Arthur B. Turnure.
*American Stained Glass*, Edward Dewson.
*Women as Art Critics*, Lillian Whiting.

The book has been produced at the large outlay of $12,000; yet it is offered to the public for the comparatively small sum of $3 a copy. The Publishers invite early and close examination of the volume, confident that it will be found the most considerable contribution yet made to the Art-literature of America, and of inestimable worth to all who are engaged in the furtherance of æsthetic culture, or in the pursuits of Art, whether Design, Painting, Sculpture, Decoration, Photography, Criticism, or in any of the various Art-manufactures and Art-industries rapidly developing amongst us.

The Publishers reserve to themselves the right of increasing the price after a certain number of copies have been sold.

CUPPLES, UPHAM & CO., Publishers,
283 Washington Street, BOSTON.

\*\*\* Mailed to any address on receipt of $3.25, postage paid.

# THE STORY OF IDA.

## By FRANCESCA.

WITH A FINE PORTRAIT FRONTISPIECE, AND AN INTRODUCTION
BY JOHN RUSKIN, D.C.L.

---

1 vol. 16mo.   Gray cloth and gilt.   Price, 75 cts.

---

THIS reprint of a little book which has been very popular in England is meeting with a warm welcome throughout the country. Its popularity is due mainly to the beauty of the story, although attention was called to it, in the first place, by Mr. Ruskin in his lectures at Oxford, and in the preface to the book. The pseudonym, "Francesca," is only a slight change of the Christian name of Miss Frances Alexander, a lady artist of Boston, now living in Florence. The great merit of her paintings won her the friendship of Mr. Ruskin, at whose urgent request "The Story of Ida"—written originally as a private memorial—was published. In his preface Mr. Ruskin says:—

"Let it be noted with thankful reverence that this is the story of a Catholic girl, written by a Protestant one, yet the two of them so united in the truth of Christian faith, and in the joy of its love, that they are absolutely unconscious of any difference in the forms or letter of their religion."

---

"'The Story of Ida' is a perfect gem of simple, unadorned narrative, and the volume is a dainty little specimen of the bookmaker's art." — BUFFALO EXPRESS.

"The story is very touching." — BOSTON ADVERTISER.

"It is tender, loving, and deeply religious." — WORCESTER SPY.

"This exquisite little story, with its preface by John Ruskin, depends for its interest upon a certain religious simplicity and refinement of thought and manners, which will commend it to those who like the works of Frances Havergal and Hesba Stretton." — BOSTON COURIER.

"The story is beautiful and touching in its simplicity, purity, and pathos, and is absolutely true in every particular." — TROY TIMES.

---

For sale by all booksellers, or mailed, postage paid, on receipt of the price,
by the publishers,

**CUPPLES, UPHAM AND COMPANY,**

283 Washington Street, Boston.

www.ingramcontent.com/pod-product-compliance
Lightning Source LLC
Chambersburg PA
CBHW020118170426
43199CB00009B/561